DRUMS ALONG BALMORAL DRIVE

BY

DOUGLAS LIVINGSTONE

E. J. Arnold & Son Ltd.
Parkside Lane
Dewsbury Road
LEEDS LS11 5TD

ISBN: 0 560-55006-5

First published 1988

Printed in Great Britain by A. Wheaton and Co. Ltd.
Hennock Road, Exeter

CONTENTS

INTRODUCTION

In 1984, a BBC producer, Brenda Reid asked me if I'd like to go to Belfast, spend a little time there, then come back and write a play about it. I did. It was called *We'll Support You Evermore* and it was well enough liked for Brenda to suggest that the BBC send me somewhere else on the same basis. We settled for Zimbabwe because 1985 was the 20th anniversary of U.D.I.

In 1965 Harold Wilson predicted that the *Unilateral Declaration of Independence* would be over in weeks rather than months, but in fact it lasted until the coming of black majority rule in 1980. It seemed to me that we had heard a lot about the British who had stayed on in India, but very little about the British who had rebelled against Britain to prevent black rule in Rhodesia — those who lost their fight and stayed on to live in Mugabe's Zimbabwe.

I read about the history of the country, books from both sides about the *War of Independence* or *The Fight Against the Terrorists*, depending which side the writer was on. I contacted those friends who had friends who could give me names and addresses to kick me off, then I flew to Harare, the capital, the place that used to be called Salisbury. (Many of the town names have been changed since Independence to rid them of colonial associations).

The flight to Harare is overnight, but the time difference, surprisingly, is only two hours, so the amount of jet-lag is small. I was booked into a rather grand hotel, the very one in which Lord Soames stayed when he was conducting the Independence negotiations. I unpacked my case and thought, *what next?* It was hot but not unpleasantly so. I put on my shorts and went for a walk in the early-Saturday-morning-city. Harare is hardly a city at all by European standards. The leafy suburbs stretch a long way, but the centre, with its occasional low skyscraper, is no more than four or five streets of mostly two storey buildings. The feel is more of Bournemouth than Africa.

I followed up my first contact: the white-run, mostly amateur theatre, *The Rep*. It spends most of the year putting on the latest West End comedy, and was just about to open with *Midsummer Night's Dream*. The contact was not there and the people at the bar had never met me, but within an hour I had been invited to a barbecue in the garden of someone's house and spent a very good day and most of the evening with the actors and backstage crew. They were all white (the only black person on the production played one of Hyppolita's servants). They had comfortable homes that could easily have been transported from Surrey, except for the flame trees in the street outside. They had black servants living in huts in their gardens. They were extremely hospitable and when they learned what I was doing — I never disguised what I was doing — they were eager to tell me about their lives and their feelings. This was the same everywhere I went. I had very few initial contacts, apart from the theatre crowd, only a black lawyer and a white judge, but they all talked openly themselves and passed me on to others who were also prepared to share their experiences.

The judge gave me the address of a lawyer in Mutare (Umtali,) a town about a hundred and fifty miles away. That lawyer took me to hear a court case, where the judges and lawyers sweated in suits and wigs, then gave me the phone number of a tea planter who invited me to stay on a remote estate. The tea planter introduced me to two English teachers at a mission school. They took me to a party given by the black headmaster and then to breakfast in a mud hut in the village. And so it went on for two weeks.

The core of the story came from a visit I made on my own to Bulawayo, the second biggest and most colonial city in Zimbabwe. I met some people in a hotel bar. Bars are an excellent place to listen; people open up when they've had a few drinks. These people invited me to their club, which is the basis for the club in the play. It was there I

5

became fascinated with the class of people who are at the centre of *Drums Along Balmoral Drive* — the less privileged whites, the lower middle class whose status depends on a society where blacks are inferior to them. Now they are having to face the reality that many blacks are moving up the social ladder passing whites like themselves on their way down.

It was not until I was back in England that I realised that these were the people I wanted to write about. By our standards, many of them were repulsive. Their racist sentiments were sometimes stronger than anything I tried to express in *Drums*. And yet I felt a tragedy there. Not a major tragedy I suppose; the long struggle of the deprived blacks is obviously a greater one.

But here was a group of people who had been taught from birth that they were superior. Their balloon had suddenly been punctured and they had no cushion of money on which to make a soft landing, nor often the intelligence to reason out the crash. I could have screamed at them, but I felt for them.

Drums is about people like them.

Douglas Livingstone

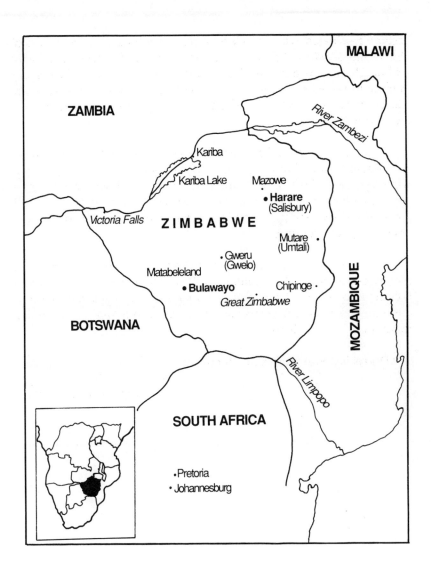

ZAMBIA

MALAWI

River Zambezi

Kariba

Kariba Lake

Mazowe

Harare
(Salisbury)

Victoria Falls

ZIMBABWE

Mutare
(Umtali)

·Gweru
(Gwelo)

Matabeleland

Bulawayo

Chipinge·

Great Zimbabwe

MOZAMBIQUE

BOTSWANA

River Limpopo

SOUTH AFRICA

·Pretoria
· Johannesburg

Harare, Zimbabwe

CAST

IN ORDER OF APPEARANCE

GEORGE BEESLEY

TAXI DRIVER

PETER BEESLEY

PIETMEYER

SARAH BEESLEY

TV VOICE OVER

TV NEWSREADER

EMMANUEL

TILLY

BRIAN

CATHY

WALLACE BADINGA

WAITER

PAUL BEESLEY

LINDA BADINGA

MICHAEL

ANDREW BADINGA

WALLACE'S FATHER

BADINGA

DRUMS ALONG BALMORAL DRIVE

SCENE 1: LONDON AIRPORT
MARCH 1986

The passengers are wrapped up against the English winter except for one man in a beige safari suit standing outside the building. He is obviously a stranger to the place. The man is GEORGE BEESLEY. He is in his mid-fifties, but looks older. He has a tanned face and the overweight figure of a man who could once have been athletic. When he speaks he has a pronounced Rhodesian accent. He leaves the terminal and gets into a taxi.

GEORGE: *(to himself)* Bloody Britain!

DRIVER: Feel the cold a bit, I bet.

GEORGE: A bit. Yes, a bit.

DRIVER: Knew where you were from soon as you opened your mouth. Rhodesia, enn'it?

GEORGE: Zimbabwe.

DRIVER: Sorry mate, no offence . . . I still call it Rhodesia. I was out there with the Air Force for a bit. National Service, you know. Late fifties. Wonderful country.

GEORGE: Oh yes. It's a wonderful country.

He looks out of the taxi window lost in thought.

DRIVER: Course, I don't talk politics . . . not wise as a cabbie . . . but there was a lot of us on your side, you know. Kith and kin, you see. Blood's thicker than water. I had a lot of time for that Ian Smith.

SCENE 2: A LONDON STREET
MARCH 1986

Two black boys play football in the road. GEORGE stands on the pavement, watching them, as his taxi moves away. He looks up and down the street of large but neglected houses in downmarket flat and bedsit country. GEORGE looks at the house in front of him then takes his bags and goes up the steps to the front door. He looks at the column of bells with their barely decipherable names beside them. Under the bells is a card in larger print than the rest, the card reads BEESLEY and has an arrow pointing towards the basement.

SCENE 3: OUTSIDE PETER'S FLAT
MARCH 1986

GEORGE presses the bell on the door of the basement flat, then waits. He seems nervous, and more so when he hears footsteps approaching the door from inside. The door opens and PETER stands in the doorway. PETER is twenty-eight. He wears a shirt and jeans and when he speaks has a Londonised Rhodesian accent. For a moment PETER can only stare.

GEORGE: Hullo Pete.

PETER: Good God.

GEORGE: Surprise, eh?

PETER: *(in disbelief)* What are you doing here?

GEORGE: I've come to see you.

SCENE 4: INSIDE PETER'S FLAT
MARCH 1986

GEORGE and PETER are in the sitting room of the small garden flat. It is a comfortable, easy-going room, furnished mainly from sales and second hand shops, but arranged and decorated with a personal style that makes it seem like a home. The sitting room doubles as dining room and the table bears the remains of PETER'S breakfast and scattered sections of the The Observer. PETER comes from the kitchenette, pulling the top from a can of beer. As he takes a glass from a shelf, he looks across at GEORGE, who sits on the sofa facing into the room, his arm resting on the arm of the sofa, but not at ease.

PETER: Sure you don't want to eat?

GEORGE: No . . . stuffed me full on the plane.

PETER: Good flight?

GEORGE: Long. Never done one as long as that.

PETER: Ah well . . . bit different from a flip down to Jo'burg.

GEORGE half-laughs. PETER hands him the can of beer and the glass.

GEORGE: Your voice has changed.

PETER: Lots of things change in ten years, Dad.

GEORGE doesn't answer. He begins to pour the beer. PETER watches. GEORGE'S hand is shaking. GEORGE pauses, then puts the partially filled glass and the can down on the small table in front of him.

          (quietly) What's the matter, Dad?

GEORGE says nothing then leans forward with his head in his hands and for a brief moment he sobs, almost silently. Then he seems to regain control and sits up again.

          What's wrong?

GEORGE: (after a moment) I don't really know where . . . don't know what . . .

He stops and picks up the little amount of beer he has managed to pour out. He takes a drink then holds the glass between his hands.

13

'Course the idea came as a shock at the time.

PETER: What did, Dad?

GEORGE: That was about . . . a month ago. Pietmeyer
                   sent for me. Don't know if you remember . . .
                   Mr Pietmeyer's the boss of the firm.

PETER: Yes. I remember.

GEORGE: I'm in charge of the workshop. Well, perhaps I
                   was when . . .

He doesn't finish.

PETER: Yes.

GEORGE: Still doing farm machinery mainly . . . sales
                   and service, you know. But given the currency
                   situation, these days it is more service than
                   sales. Anyway, this day he sent for me, Mr
                   Pietmeyer did.

SCENE 5: MR PIETMEYER'S OFFICE.
FLASHBACK FEBRUARY 1986

*A calendar on the wall behind the desk of the comfortable, but functional
office has a picture of Harare City Centre and announces,* Invicta
Engineering, Harare. *PIETMEYER, a heavy man, probably older than
GEORGE, sits behind his desk in the office. He is wearing shorts and a
safari shirt.*

PIETMEYER: Come in.

GEORGE comes into the office. He too is wearing shorts and safari shirt.

                   Oh hullo, George. How are you?

GEORGE: Not too bad, Sir.

14

PIETMEYER:	Good. Sit down.

GEORGE sits down at the other side of the desk.

	(offering a packet) Cigarette?
GEORGE:	Given them up, Sir.
PIETMEYER:	Wish I had! No I don't . . . ridiculous! If everyone gave up smoking what would happen to the country's economy, eh?
GEORGE:	What has happened to it, Sir?

PIETMEYER looks at him.

PIETMEYER:	You sound like a man who's looking for out. Any plans?
GEORGE:	Mr Pietmeyer, as you know I have had plans to get out since the day they elected bloody Mugabe. Where I fancy going I can't afford to live, where I might just afford it, I don't want to go!

He smiles.

	Have no fears about me, Sir, you're stuck with me till the day I retire!
PIETMEYER:	*(pause)* I've sold up, George. I'm going South.

GEORGE stares at him.

	Sorry to break it to you like this. Couldn't risk it getting out till I got the right price. Course, with these government regulations, I can't get the money out for a few years . . . but my son's in business down in Jo'burg and we've made an arrangement and I should be all right.

15

GEORGE:	You should be all right? What about me?
PIETMEYER:	Oh, I don't think you'll have to worry, George. For a start, Mr Badinga says . . .
GEORGE:	Badinga?
PIETMEYER:	Mr Badinga has bought the firm. Oh don't worry, it's not that Badinga . . . not Comrade Badinga . . . this is a . . . distant nephew of his.
GEORGE:	*(looking at him)* You've sold out to an Af.
PIETMEYER:	It's the Africans' country nowadays, George.
GEORGE:	And that's why you're bloody getting out!
PIETMEYER:	Mr Badinga says he has no objection to keeping the staff more or less as it is.
GEORGE:	Kiss his arse . . . many thanks.
PIETMEYER:	He'll want to talk to you, of course . . . but I'm sure there'll be no problem there. And if there should be, by some chance . . . I mean if you don't happen to see eye to eye, no problem either . . . not for you. You're a good worker . . . you're a skilled man . . . you'll find something easy enough.
GEORGE:	For God's sake, Sir, I'm fifty four!
PIETMEYER:	*(quietly)* I'm sorry, George.

SCENE 6: PETER'S FLAT
MARCH 1986

GEORGE still sits on the sofa. PETER sits on a chair at the table, watching him. Suddenly GEORGE looks round.

GEORGE: Nice room this.

PETER: Thank you. Most of the decoration's done by Trish.

GEORGE: Trish?

PETER: The girl I live with nowadays.

GEORGE: Oh.

PETER: I put her name on last year's Christmas card.

GEORGE: Oh, that's right, yes. I'm afraid you didn't get a Christmas card.

PETER doesn't comment.

PETER: She's visiting her parents this weekend.

GEORGE'S eye catches sight of something.

GEORGE: Good Lord.

PETER: What?

GEORGE gets up and goes towards a framed photograph on the mantelpiece.

GEORGE: Our house.

PETER: Yes.

The photograph shows PETER, looking considerably younger, another boy, a little older than PETER, and SARAH, GEORGE'S wife, sitting beside a small swimming pool. Behind them is a neat bungalow.

GEORGE: I took that picture. Did a lot of work on that pool, too! Nice house, isn't it, Pete?

PETER: Oh yes.

GEORGE: Nice road, Balmoral Drive. Not the very best part of Harare . . . even I don't call it Salisbury now . . . not the best part . . . out of our bracket . . . but very nice. Very nice. Flame trees in the street, decent bit of ground, decent set of neighbours. Very nice. Not the sort of thing you want to give up. Not without an effort, anyway.

PETER: Have you given it up?

SCENE 7: GEORGE AND SARAH'S HOUSE
FLASHBACK FEBRUARY 1986

It is evening. In the lounge a black and white television set is on. A precise, near-English, female voice can be heard over the advertising caption showing a drawing of a plane and a ship and the name Bradstock and Co. Machel Avenue. Harare. *SARAH is sitting in a chair, a drink in her hand. She is watching the television. SARAH is in her fifties. Both her dress and her hairstyle have a slightly old-fashioned provincial English look. With the exception of the overhead fan, the furnishings and decor of the room could be suburban Surrey, thirty years ago.*

TV VOICE: **Hullo. Are you considering emigration? Are you daunted by legalities and paperwork? Why not consult the experts now? For emigration, or immigration, Bradstock and Company can smooth your path. For emigration made easy, consult Bradstock. Why not call us now?**

GEORGE: 'Evening.

SARAH looks round to see that GEORGE has come into the room.

SARAH: Oh hullo, George. Good day?

GEORGE: *(shrugging)* Pretty usual.

She gets up and goes towards the drinks trolley.

SARAH: I'll get you a drink. Oh George, we're out of
                     ice.

GEORGE: *(calling)* Emmanuel . . . ice!

*SARAH continues to the trolley on which the drinks are kept. The
AFRICAN NEWSREADER is now on the television screen. GEORGE'S
eyes go to the set.*

NEWSREADER: Good evening. In Harare today, the Prime
                     Minister, Comrade Robert Mugabe, said that
                     the economy of the country was now in a
                     much healthier state.

A picture of Mugabe comes on to the screen.

                     Comrade Mugabe was speaking . . .

SARAH: Kill the Comrade, George.

NEWSREADER: . . . at a meeting of the economics committee
                     of the O.A.U., Comrade Mugabe —

GEORGE switches off the set. She glances at him as he does so.

SARAH: So what happened?

GEORGE: *(nervously)* Er . . . oh, it's tomorrow.

SARAH: What is?

GEORGE: Badinga.

SARAH: What d'you mean?

GEORGE: I see him tomorrow.

SARAH: What about?

GEORGE: *(half-laughs)* I mean about the job.

SARAH looks at GEORGE.

SARAH: George . . . you asked me . . .

*She stops as EMMANUEL comes in with the ice. EMMANUEL is
probably in his late twenties, he wears a shirt and long baggy shorts.*

EMMANUEL: Ice, Sir.

GEORGE: Oh thank you, Emmanuel.

SARAH: There's a dirty glass here, Emmanuel . . . you
                 know I hate dirty glasses.

EMMANUEL: Sorry, Missus.

She hands him the offending glass.

SARAH: Wipe them properly when you've washed
                 them.

EMMANUEL: Sorry Missus. Missus, my cousin stay the
                 night. Is OK, Missus?

SARAH: I suppose so, yes. But just one night.

EMMANUEL: Thank you, Missus.

He goes out.

GEORGE:	God knows how they manage with three in that hut.
SARAH:	Look George, we talked about this job last night. You asked me what I thought and I . . .
GEORGE:	*(interrupting her)* Will you leave it, Sarah, please! *(pause)* I'm sorry, but I'm the one who has to make the living. How I do it is up to me.

She doesn't reply, instead she takes him his drink.

	Thank you. Cheers.
SARAH:	Don't forget we're at the club tonight. It's ballroom night.

SCENE 8: THE CLUB BAR
FLASHBACK FEBRUARY 1986

The club is a wooden pavilion-like building and its decor has seen better times. The bar of the club is rather crudely decorated in mock-tudor style. Above the bar counter is a sign announcing Tally-Ho Bar, *and the surrounds of the bar itself are decorated with faded pictures of English hunting scenes. Middle-aged and elderly couples can be seen dancing, in a fairly stately way, to a dance band version of* On The Street Where You Live, *being played on a gramophone. A French window leads to a small enclosed terrace, lit by fairy lights, several of the bulbs of which are missing. There seems to be no more than a dozen people in the club.*

GEORGE'S VOICE:	'Course you remember ballroom nights. You learned to dance at ballroom nights. Not what they were. Sometimes you get so few on the floor you feel a twerp getting up to dance. Still, I like the Tally-Ho. Not one of the poshest Harare clubs . . . but suits us, we like it, always have.

21

| GEORGE: | *(to the black BARMAN)* One Castle, One Lion, two brandy and soda. |
| TILLY: | George. |

GEORGE turns to see TILLY sitting on a stool at the bar near him. TILLY is a little younger than SARAH, but has the same old-fashioned look. A similar woman sits beside TILLY.

GEORGE:	Oh hullo, Tilly.
TILLY:	George, you don't know where I can buy fish paste, do you?
GEORGE:	Fish paste?
TILLY:	I was saying to Jane, you cannot buy fish paste in this country anymore. If I want a jar of fish paste today, I have to wait till I visit my daughter down South.

As TILLY'S talk continues to hit GEORGE'S ears, he takes a book of tickets from his pocket. The tickets are printed to be used as substitute money and GEORGE begins to tear some out to pay for the drinks.

	I mean, all through the war you could buy fish paste. Sanctions or not you could still get fish paste.
GEORGE:	I don't like fish paste.
TILLY:	Nor does Frank. But I love fish paste.

GEORGE has put down the appropriate number of tickets and now picks up the tray of drinks.

| GEORGE: | S'cuse me, Tilly. |
| TILLY: | Oh George, tell the girls I've got a cake sale |

Saturday. For the Mission School. Ask them to do me some of their specials.

GEORGE: Right. *(moving away)*

TILLY turns back to the other woman.

TILLY: My speciality used to be almond cake . . . but it's so hard to get . . .

GEORGE moves past a poster advertising an amateur performance of The Pirates of Penzance *and out of earshot of TILLY. He then goes through the French windows to the terrace.*

SCENE 9: THE CLUB TERRACE
FLASHBACK FEBRUARY 1986

SARAH, CATHY and BRIAN are the only people occupying a table on the small terrace. BRIAN is an ex-rugby player in his early fifties. CATHY is a bit younger than her husband.

GEORGE: *(arriving with the tray)* Here we are then.

BRIAN: Well done, George.

GEORGE: *(putting down the drinks)* I'm afraid Tilly's on the cake warpath. Wants some of your specials.

CATHY: Oh Gawd.

SARAH: Mission school?

GEORGE: Yes.

SARAH: Oh well . . . good cause.

CATHY: Oh yes. *(to BRIAN)* We're trying to buy them a trampoline.

BRIAN:	*(for want of something to say)* Oh.
SARAH:	George, you haven't asked Cathy to dance, tonight.
GEORGE:	Blimey, I've just got a beer. Cathy, d'you want to dance?
SARAH:	What sort of invitation's that?
CATHY:	He'd only tread on my toes. George, drink your beer.
BRIAN:	Don't be rude about George. He was club champion, 'fore I married you . . . when were you and Sarah club champions, George?
SARAH:	'65, '66, '70, '72. It's up there on the board.
GEORGE:	That board needs a repaint . . . it's hardly readable.
SARAH:	The whole place needs a repaint. And this chair needs mending. Dismiss the committee!
BRIAN:	Dismiss the committee any day you like . . . you try and find someone else to serve! I'll tell you very easy how we paint this place . . . we straight away double the subscription.
GEORGE:	Oh yes . . . thank you.
BRIAN:	And throw open the membership.
SARAH:	And we know what that means, thank you very much.
GEORGE:	They wouldn't want to come here anyway.
SARAH:	I bet a thousand dollars they would.

GEORGE:	They've got places of their own. They've got lively places.
SARAH:	Oh don't be daft, George. Whatever else they are, they're snobs . . . give their gold teeth for a membership card here.
GEORGE:	For the polo club, maybe . . . don't know about here.
BRIAN:	The polo club doesn't need 'em . . . and if they did they could afford to take 'em . . . at their prices they'd only get their crème de la crème.
CATHY:	(giggling) Crème de la crème. I think you mean their noir de la noir.
BRIAN:	(not laughing) Yes, very good, yes. What I'm saying is they wouldn't lose their standards. If we said the membership list was open, we'd get all sorts of riff-raff applying here. And you couldn't turn them down . . . not without asking for trouble.
CATHY:	As Brian is always saying, aren't you, Brian . . . it's our sort gets the worst of every deal.
BRIAN:	You wouldn't think it to hear the fat cats go on. I was out the Mazowe Valley today . . . tobacco farmer complaining to hell about the new Mercedes he's bringing in. *Isn't it hard on poor me*, he says, *I've got to pay 20,000 thousand dollars in import tax.* I thought, I'm shedding no tears for you, if you hadn't got the twenty thou, not to mention the price of the Merc, you wouldn't be importing it. Don't know they're born, some of these farmers.
GEORGE:	Fat whites, fat blacks in each other's pockets.

BRIAN:	Course they are. And the Government. *Comrade this . . . Comrade bloody that . . .* They're all buying hotels in Switzerland.
SARAH:	Especially Badinga.
GEORGE:	*(warningly)* Sarah.
BRIAN:	*(not hearing GEORGE)* Huh, Badinga. That little sod.
SARAH:	He's not only buying in Switzerland . . . he's buying up half of Harare as well.
GEORGE:	Sarah, I said . . . not tonight . . . please.
SARAH:	They're our friends, George. We've no secrets from them.
GEORGE:	It is not a secret.
SARAH:	In which case there's no reason they shouldn't know.

BRIAN and CATHY are all ears, but are too polite to enquire. GEORGE sighs and gives in.

GEORGE:	Pietmeyer's sold the firm. He's going South.
SARAH:	He's sold it to Badinga.
BRIAN:	Christ.
GEORGE:	It's not that Badinga . . . it's his nephew.
SARAH:	It's his money. The nephew's a front.
GEORGE:	We don't know that.
SARAH:	Oh come on, George, of course it is. Where

26

	would the nephew get the money from?
BRIAN:	So what's happening to you, George?
CATHY:	Are you staying on?
SARAH:	Well he can't, can he! He can't work for that terr. He's not going round saying *Sir* to him.
CATHY:	What you going to do then?
SARAH:	Go South. We'll have to.
GEORGE:	*(sharply)* There is nothing decided!

He calms himself.

	Sorry. There's nothing decided. I'm meeting him tomorrow. Have a talk. Test the water. I daresay Sarah's absolutely right . . . but I'd be a fool not to test the water. Well, wouldn't I?
BRIAN:	*(unconvincingly)* Oh yes.

SCENE 10: PETER'S FLAT
MARCH 1986

GEORGE and PETER are sitting as before. GEORGE is not looking at PETER and it is almost as if he is talking to himself. PETER watches him.

GEORGE:	They didn't mean it, of course. But then it wasn't them. Easy for Brian. His job was safe. He wouldn't do it. He wouldn't kowtow. Well one day he might bloody well have to. Anyway, nobody treads on me. I'm my own man . . . make up my own mind. I've a lot of time for the African. I'm telling you, your best African is among the very best of men. He's not like us . . . doesn't want to be . . . we do

not want to be like him. We have our standards, he has his. They're not the same standards . . . never will be. I don't want to chuck my standards. Soon have to, wouldn't I, without a job. Anyway, I didn't know Badinga. Not his fault his uncle was a terrorist! Half of 'em were terrorists. Never knew who they were. The black in your workshop. Bring you coffee in the day . . . shooting at you in the bush at night . . . then smiling and bringing you coffee next morning. How could you tell who the hell was a terr? Mind you Badinga wasn't just a terr. When that plane was shot down from Victoria Falls . . . when those women survivors were raped and shot, Badinga went on Zambian television and when they asked him about it, he smiled.

PETER: He says he didn't smile.

GEORGE: *(pointing a finger)* He smiled!

PETER: I remember the announcers on Rhodesian telly used to look pretty pleased when they said terrs were killed.

GEORGE: Don't start that, please . . . don't start it! I haven't come here to argue with you. I've argued with you. I'm not arguing now.

He looks away. There is a slight pause.

GEORGE: So anyway . . . anyway . . . Wallace . . . that's his name . . . Wallace Badinga. Told me to call him Wallace. Didn't see me in an office. Took me to lunch.

SCENE 11: MEIKLES HOTEL
FLASHBACK FEBRUARY 1986

WALLACE BADINGA is a young African, probably in his late twenties or early thirties. He is sitting at a table in the dining room of Meikles Hotel. He is wearing a well cut dark suit. GEORGE who sits opposite him, wears a lightweight linen suit. Less well cut. WALLACE'S accent is quite light, and his manner, always pleasant, varies between the boyishly eager and the laid back. Both he and GEORGE have glasses of beer in front of them. A WAITER stands beside the table.

WALLACE:	And I'll have a sirloin steak . . . medium rare . . . a chef's salad, french dressing . . . and a few sauté potatoes! *(he smiles at GEORGE)* Why not!
WAITER:	Nothing to start, Sir?
WALLACE:	No thank you.
GEORGE:	Oh well . . . in that case.
WALLACE:	Don't be silly, George . . . you wanted a starter, you shall have one! I have only a one course appetite. Now, to drink. How does the mood take you, George? Wine or more beer?
GEORGE:	*(uncomfortably)* I think I'll stick to beer, please?
WALLACE:	*(to the WAITER)* Two more Castles.
WAITER:	Sir.

He goes.

WALLACE:	I do like this hotel. I hear it is now rated one of the best in the world. But you will have been here often, of course.
GEORGE:	Only to functions. In the Functions Room.

WALLACE:	Oh, you've not tried the restaurant? Well, I'm sure you'll like the food. I'm sure you'll come back. Anyway, it's good to have lunch. I like the European habit of business lunch. Much more civilised than across the desk in an office. Here you get to know somebody man to man. *(he smiles)* So to business, eh?

GEORGE in the act of picking up his glass, hesitates.

	No, carry on, please. Obviously, George, I know quite a lot about you. The personal file facts. And I've talked around. People like you. You're a popular man.
GEORGE:	*(awkwardly)* Well . . . hope so.
WALLACE:	Oh yes, yes. But you should know about me . . . and you know very little. My facts. In brief. I was born near Chipinge. Educated at Mount Selinda . . . then at Mutare. In 1976 I went to London and took a degree in Economics. I liked London very much. Rather dirty, but very exciting. Do you like London, George?
GEORGE:	I've never been to London. Never been to UK.
WALLACE:	Good Heavens, I thought you all called it home.
GEORGE:	I call this country home.
WALLACE:	That's very good, George. Back to me then. I am now a married man and we have one child. My uncle is a government minister, my father is a business man. I have experience in various commerical firms and now I have persuaded my father . . . and one or two other businessmen to put up the money to

purchase Invicta. At this moment I would call the firm archaic. A rather self-satisfied one man band. Pietmeyer has his contacts and does business with them. It gives him a comfortable standard of living, it pays his wages bill and that's the end. The firm is dead as a dodo. Would you agree?

GEORGE doesn't answer.

George?

GEORGE: It has a . . . solid reputation . . . among the farmers.

WALLACE: Tactfully put. I do not plan to destroy that reputation. I have a solid body . . . I shall bring it to life. Expansion . . . expansion! I am ambitious, George. I mean to succeed.

The drinks WAITER arrives with the beer.

WAITER: Beer, Sir.

WALLACE: Thank you.

The WAITER goes to put down a bottle beside WALLACE. WALLACE raises his hand to indicate that GEORGE should be served first.

GEORGE: Thank you.

The WAITER goes. GEORGE looks at WALLACE as WALLACE pours his beer.

So . . . um . . . so you'd want me to stay on in the old job, would you?

WALLACE: No. *(he looks at GEORGE)* Not the old job. Look at Invicta now. Pietmeyer behind the desk, or out around the farms, you taking his orders and bossing the workshop. I know very good African mechanics who would boss the workshop as well as you.

GEORGE: Oh. I'm sorry. I thought you wanted me to stay.

WALLACE: I want to put a proposition to you.

The WAITER arrives and offers a plate of smoked fish to GEORGE.

GEORGE: Oh, thank you.

The WAITER goes.

WALLACE: Please carry on.

GEORGE has no alternative but to eat alone, feeling he is being watched as he tackles the rather bony fish.

I want to put a proposition to you.

GEORGE: Yes?

WALLACE: You know what Robert says?

GEORGE: Robert?

WALLACE: Mugabe.

GEORGE: Oh.

WALLACE: How is the fish? Good?

GEORGE: Oh yes . . . fine thank you.

WALLACE: Robert says the white issue is dead. It no longer exists. And, of course, he is right. In my experience Robert usually is. When he says it is dead, he means the question of black

or white rule is dead. The issue is settled . . .
majority rule. We are one nation, he says, OK
there is a little trouble in Matabeleland . . .
but that will be settled sooner than later. As
far as black and white is concerned we must
have reconciliation, he says. It is a wonderful
thing to say and does the world give him
credit enough for it? The war was bitter and
ugly and very many were killed. There was
cruelty and atrocities on both sides. Hatred on
both sides. And what happens when
Comrade Mugabe wins? The first thing he
commands is *No Revenge.* Reconciliation. It is
a wonderful thing to say. The most important
statement ever made in this country. Don't
you think so, George?

GEORGE: *(uncomfortably)* Oh yes . . . yes.

WALLACE: And very sensible.

GEORGE: Yes.

WALLACE: If I seem to be straying, I am not. I am coming
towards the proposition. So reconciliation is
the name of the game and reconciliation is
beginning to work. But I am a realist. I see
things as they are. Of course there will always
be black and white. Men were not,
unfortunately, born colour blind. I go further
though. I understand the suspicion that still
exists. I put myself in your position . . . not
your position personally, George, your
position as a colonist, I mean. I put myself in
your position . . . you come here ninety years
ago . . . your country sends you . . . they urge
you on. *The world is better British . . . follow
Cecil Rhodes.* You work like hell . . . you
cultivate the land . . . you make a colony that
King and country cheer . . . then suddenly . . .

(he snaps his fingers) I'm sorry fellows, we were having you on. The country's not yours as we said it would be . . . it belongs to the black man . . . hand it over now. I wouldn't like it . . . why should you?

He smiles.

Put yourself in my position. Not mine personally. A hundred years ago my people lived on the land . . . hunting fishing, enjoying life. Then suddenly the ox-carts roll and along comes the white man. Not crude. Not bang-bang, off you go. But . . . *We are here to improve your life. Move on to those reservations, leave us the best land; our missionaries will teach you the Bible . . . and if you want to earn a crust then, OK . . . you come and slave for us.*

GEORGE: *(impatiently)* Look, I'm very sorry, Mr Badinga, I didn't realise I was here for a history lesson. I thought I was here so I could discuss whether or not I worked for you!

WALLACE looks at him, then takes a drink of beer.

WALLACE: Believe me, George, that's what we are here discussing. I wanted to explain to you that, even given the process of reconciliation . . . I understand the resentment that still exists. I must if I am to run a successful business. It comes out in big ways, it comes out in small. You say, not you personally, George . . . you say Robert Mugabe is pinching the taxes to build hotels in Switzerland. You say black men eat with their mouths open . . . and don't know how to use a lavatory. We say that white men here still live off the fat . . . and their wives have long faces . . . because their men have small cocks.

They look at each other. WALLACE sniggers, then GEORGE cannot help doing the same.

I don't believe that, of course.

They both laugh quietly.

So that's the proposition, George.

GEORGE: What is?

WALLACE: If I am realistic about this country today . . .
                 and if I wish to build this firm as I wish to
                 build it . . . then I need new clients, many of
                 whom will be white. If I provide a white man
                 to deal with these white clients, then these
                 white clients will feel more at ease.

He looks at GEORGE and smiles.

How would you like to be my white man,
George?

SCENE 12: PETER'S FLAT
MARCH 1986

GEORGE gets up from his seat, walks over to the mantelpiece and looks closely at the photograph of PETER, PAUL and SARAH, round the swimming pool. He turns and looks across at PETER, who is waiting for him to continue. Their eyes meet for a moment and then GEORGE returns to his seat.

SCENE 13: THE CLUB
FLASHBACK 1976

It is evening; a group of young soldiers including PAUL, GEORGE and

SARAH'S son are standing at the bar with bottles of beer, singing. The bar is decorated with Rhodesian flags and a large picture of Smith hangs behind the singers. GEORGE and SARAH, both looking nine or ten years younger, are standing nearby and joining in the singing. Other club members are also singing enthusiastically.

SOLDIERS:	*(singing)* It's a long way to Mukemburra, It's a long way to brawl, It's a long way to Mukemburra But you can have yourself a ball!

GEORGE looks across the bar to where PETER, in civilian clothes, sits at a table watching. PETER catches his father's eye and forces himself to smile.

SOLDIERS:	*(singing)* Goodbye, Bulawayo, Doysha Cecil Square, It's a long long way to Mukemburra, But there's terrs to kill right there!

Everyone except PETER cheers.

PAUL:	Give me an R!
OTHERS:	*(shouting)* R!
PAUL:	Give me an H.
OTHERS:	H.
PAUL:	Give me an O.
OTHERS:	O.
PAUL:	Give me a D.
OTHERS:	D.
PAUL:	*(with increasing speed)*Give me an E, give me an S, give me an I, an A . . .

36

ALL: *(shouting)* Rhodesia

SCENE 14: GEORGE AND SARAH'S HOUSE
FLASHBACK FEBRUARY 1986

A framed photograph of PAUL wearing army uniform stands on an occasional table near the drinks trolley. In the lounge Sarah is pouring drinks. George stands in the room watching her.

GEORGE: I liked him.

She says nothing.

                        (qualifying) I mean, he's a typical educated Af . . . bit full of himself . . . bit I-know-it-all . . . but on the whole not too bad. I reckon I could work with him.

SARAH: For him.

She turns to him and hands him his drink.

GEORGE: Ooh . . . better be careful. Still feeling what I had lunch time. He insisted on brandies after the meal.

SARAH: Must show off, mustn't they. Ten years ago he wouldn't dare set foot in Meikles Hotel.

GEORGE: It's not ten years ago.

SARAH: Don't lecture me, George . . . I'm aware of that. Anyway, you told him no.

GEORGE: I did not tell him no! For Christ's sake, how could I tell him no!

SARAH: Please watch your language.

GEORGE:	Look Sarah . . . he's offering me a raise of twenty five per cent . . . plus a nice commission on the business I make. He's offering me the chance to get out of that workshop . . . go round the country, selling, making contacts. He's even suggesting I might get abroad.
SARAH:	Lucky you.
GEORGE:	I'll be part of this firm for the first time, Sarah. I won't just be what I always have . . . a foreman who picks up a salary cheque . . . It's a big chance . . . big chance . . . I've got to think about it.

She laughs quietly.

	What's the matter?
SARAH:	I was just remembering the way you went on in '82 when Chris Anderssen walked out on Smithy and joined Mugabe's Government. He's a white Uncle Tom, that's what you said. You wanted to hang him.
GEORGE:	It's not the same thing at all.
SARAH:	Oh isn't it?
GEORGE:	No.
SARAH:	Joining up with the murderers, you said.

He sighs.

	You're joining with the people who murdered your son.

He looks at her, then turns away. Suddenly she snatches up the photograph

38

of PAUL and smashes it into the fireplace.

GEORGE: *(after a moment)* What d'you do that for?

SARAH: Because I felt like it.

He goes to the fireplace and begins to pick up the photograph and the remains of the glass.

                      I'm sorry. I felt like it.

SARAH looks at GEORGE clearing up.

                      Leave that. Emmanuel'll do it.

GEORGE: Do you want him to know all our business?

SARAH: What of it, d'you think he doesn't know?

GEORGE puts the glassless photograph back on the table.

GEORGE: Paul was in the army . . . he was fighting a
                      war.

SARAH: That's not what you said when they brought
                      him home.

GEORGE: You can't carry on blaming every black in this
                      country.

SARAH: I can blame Badinga. You often have.

GEORGE: I'm not working for Badinga . . . not that
                      Badinga.

SARAH: Wasn't this one in the war?

GEORGE: I don't know. I didn't ask him. We were
                      talking about work, not the bloody war.

39

SARAH:	Oh I see . . . the famous *reconciliation*.
GEORGE:	*(breaking)* No! Bread and butter. Cash. Dollars. Rands. Pounds, shillings and pence! *(slight pause)* Look, I'm sorry, Sarah, but this has got to be said . . . it's no good living in cloud cuckoo land. *Go South,* you say . . . *go South.* I wouldn't mind going South. I like Jo'burg. I like the Cape. But facts is facts . . . we can't afford to go South. Jim Forster went South, he had to come back. The cost of living down there is out of sight. What d'you think we'd get if we sold this place? Thirty five thousand dollars very top whack. It's a buyer's market here . . . everybody's selling . . . down South you couldn't buy a shack for that. Anyway, I couldn't get the money out . . . not for four years I couldn't . . . I mean what d'you think we'd live on till then? There's unemployment down there . . . I couldn't get a job . . . we'd have my bit of pension and that'd be that. We've got a standard up here . . . we eat well, drink well . . . we've got a houseboy . . . we've got a pool. Down South we'd just be poor whites. Trash. Is that what you fancy? I know I don't. All right, so what about UK? The way those buggers let us down, I wouldn't set one foot in UK . . . and even if I would there's nothing there for us. You think we'd get something like our style of life? Two rooms and the dole, that's us in UK . . . we are stuck here. Stuck. No alternative. I'm sorry, Sarah, but these are the *facts*.

There is a silence. She drinks.

SARAH:	Yes. Yes, I'm being ridiculous.
GEORGE:	I didn't say that.

SARAH:	Anyway, it's silly to be arguing. You've said yes and that's it.
GEORGE:	Look, I haven't said yes. For God's sake, you're right . . . it's both of us. There's nothing decided. It's not even offered yet.
SARAH:	Not offered? What d'you mean?
GEORGE:	I mean, he wants to meet you first.
SARAH:	Me?
GEORGE:	He says there'll be entertaining to do. Have people here . . . take clients and their wives to restaurants. A wife's very important in that, he said. He wants to meet you.
SARAH:	Look me over, you mean?
GEORGE:	I'm sure it's not that. He just wants to meet you. He's quite understanding of things in a way . . . he understands our problems in working for him. I suppose he wants to make sure you'd back me in it.

She says nothing.

I think what we must do is . . . meet him . . . both of us . . . and if at the end of it you do decide . . . after weighing it all up . . . if you do decide no . . . then even if he offers it . . . we'll have to think again. Find some sort of other job here perhaps. Won't be much. Not what he's suggesting. But it might just about keep us going.

SARAH:	*(quietly)* Where we meeting him? Meikles?
GEORGE:	*(uncomfortably)* No. We're going to his place.

41

SARAH:	His place?
GEORGE:	On Saturday.
SARAH:	We can't go Saturday . . . we're going to the lake with Cathy and Brian.
GEORGE:	Sod the lake. Sod Cathy and Brian. We're going to his place!
SARAH:	*(quietly)* I'm sorry. Yes. All right.
GEORGE:	It's his son's birthday. They're having a party. They've invited us to it.
SARAH:	*(after a slight pause)* Sounds very nice.

She moves away to pour herself another drink. GEORGE watches her.

GEORGE'S VOICE: **I don't know what happened between then and Saturday. We didn't talk about it again . . . not really. Perhaps she just thought over what I said. Weighed the alternatives, decided I was right. Anyway, whatever it was, come Saturday she seemed to have changed. She'd had her hair done, bought a new dress. Even started to chivvy me.**

SCENE 15: GEORGE AND SARAH'S HOUSE
FLASHBACK FEBRUARY 1986

GEORGE and SARAH'S bedroom is in conventional English style and is dominated by a heavy double bed. It is Saturday and daytime. SARAH is sitting at the dressing table making up her face. GEORGE is in the background putting on his jacket.

SARAH:	Your other jacket's clean.
GEORGE:	What's the matter with this one?

SARAH:	You've put on a bit of weight since you bought that. You look younger in the other one.
GEORGE:	Oh, all right.

He takes the other jacket from the wardrobe.

	You look nice in that dress.
SARAH:	Thank you.
GEORGE:	D'you know something very odd. I've never been in an African's house before. Except when I was doing police reserve.
SARAH:	Don't think you'd better mention that. Anyway, it'll hardly be a mud hut, will it, George! Not on Tennyson Drive. The Franklins lived there before they went to UK. I'm sure it'll be very nice.
GEORGE'S VOICE:	**And it was very nice. Very nice. And, give him his due . . . he was very nice.**

SCENE 16: WALLACE BADINGA'S HOUSE
FLASHBACK FEBRUARY 1986

WALLACE is greeting GEORGE and SARAH in the lounge of his neo-colonial house. The furniture is a mixture of Harare-European and Europeanised-African. There are about a dozen other guests, all African. The men are in European casual clothes, and the women are in brightly coloured dresses. GEORGE nervously watches SARAH through the introductions.

WALLACE:	Mrs Beesley, so good of you to come.
SARAH:	*(only a little gracious)* I'm very pleased to meet you, Mr Badinga.

43

WALLACE:	Please call me Wallace. I asked George to do the same. And you are?
SARAH:	Sarah.
WALLACE:	Sarah. *(to SARAH)* May I call you that?
SARAH:	Of course.
WALLACE:	We had planned to have the party round the pool . . . but it has already rained once and I fear it may do so again.
SARAH:	It was very good for the crops. They need it.
WALLACE:	Precisely the way I look at it . . . Now Sarah, may I introduce my wife?

He calls to a pretty woman in her twenties.

Linda. Come and meet Sarah and George.

LINDA crosses to them.

This is my wife . . . Linda . . . Sarah, George.

LINDA'S accent is more pronounced than WALLACE'S.

LINDA:	How do you do?
SARAH:	Pleased to meet you.
GEORGE:	Pleased to meet you.

They shake hands, then SARAH hands over a gift-wrapped parcel.

SARAH:	This is for your son.
LINDA:	You're very kind. He is playing with his

	friends in the garden. I will give it to him.
SARAH:	You have a very nice house, Linda.
WALLACE:	We bought it from some people who are going back to UK, Littlehampton. A very reasonable price.
SARAH:	It's a buyer's market.
WALLACE:	Oh yes. Anyway, it is certainly different from Linda's last house . . . which is over here.

He smiles and leads them to a framed photograph on the wall. In the photograph a man, a woman and two children are standing in front of a mud hut.

I'm afraid the photograph is slightly out of focus. I took it after drinking Maganu. Terrible stuff. The widows have the right to brew it, you know. It gives them some money and gives us bad heads. They say if you put it in a metal bowl it will rot it right through in twenty four hours.

He points to the people.

This is Stanley, Linda's brother, and his wife and children. He is a teacher. We need all the teachers we can get. Teachers and birth control.

He laughs. GEORGE and SARAH join in, if rather awkwardly.

Have you ever been in a mud hut, George?

| GEORGE: | No I haven't no. |
| WALLACE: | Not even when you were doing police reserve? |

GEORGE: *(embarrassed)* Well, I saw in them then . . . but not really . . . um . . .

WALLACE: They're surprisingly comfortable. But the termites destroy the framework in five years or so and you have to build yourself another one. Stanley is constructing a brick hut now . . . they last a big longer.

GEORGE: S'pose so.

SARAH: Lovely baby.

WALLACE: Oh yes. If babies have enough in their bellies they're usually lovely . . . and content. We have a long way to go, but we're working at it!

WALLACE indicates the room in which they're standing.

A long way to go with housing as well . . . a small step for this man, a big leap for mankind!

He laughs again, and again the others join in.

Now let me introduce you to some of my friends.

LINDA: Will you excuse me, I must supervise the food.

SARAH: Of course.

GEORGE: Oh yes.

WALLACE: Come over here and meet Michael and Rosie.

He leads them towards a young couple.

Michael . . . Rose. This is Sarah and George.

46

MICHAEL:	Ah . . . pleased to meet you.
GEORGE:	How d'you do?
SARAH:	How d'you do?
MICHAEL:	What a pity about the rain.
GEORGE:	Yes, it is, isn't it.
MICHAEL:	Still . . . good for the farmers.
SARAH:	That's what I was saying.

★   ★   ★

We hear GEORGE'S voice over a background of party chatter and laughter. SARAH is smiling and shaking hands with other guests. GEORGE is watching SARAH. SARAH is drinking, smiling, shaking hands again. Her smile is never quite perfect and the handshake never quite full-blooded, but as far as GEORGE is concerned, they are more than satisfactory.

GEORGE'S VOICE: **And she was doing very well. Very well. Better than I was in many ways. And his uncle wasn't there, so that was all right . . . but we seemed to meet everyone who was. And they all seemed to like her . . . well, no reason why they shouldn't. And they were charming to her . . . charming. Well, no reason why they shouldn't be, of course.**

★   ★   ★

Music is now playing and for a moment GEORGE and SARAH have no one else with them.

GEORGE:	*(smiling)* Like a normal party, isn't it?
SARAH:	Yes.

LINDA: *(approaching with a plate)* Would you care for
                          one of these. They are home-made.

*GEORGE looks at the rather strange looking fried cakes on the plate. The
pause is just long enough for SARAH to notice.*

SARAH: *(rescuing him)* Oh may I have one?

LINDA: Yes, of course.

WALLACE   *(passing)* Ah, must try one of those, George . . .
                          Linda's speciality.

GEORGE: Oh well, of course I must, yes!

GEORGE takes one.

                          Thank you.

LINDA: Excuse me.

GEORGE: Of course.

Linda moves on, for another moment GEORGE and SARAH are alone.

                          (quietly) What the hell's this?

SARAH: Well it has to be eaten.

She bites into her cake. He watches her, she shows no reaction at all.

                          Go on.

GEORGE bites and eats.

WALLACE: *(passing again)* Good, George?

GEORGE: *(his mouth full)* Excellent.

WALLACE: Plenty more over there . . . help yourselves.

GEORGE: Thank you.

He is about to move on, then puts his arm round GEORGE'S shoulder.

WALLACE: D'you like television George?

He indicates a large colour TV set which is showing a Wombles *cartoon, but with the sound turned down.*

GEORGE: Very nice.

WALLACE: *(confidentially)* I only keep it on to prove that it's colour . . . impress the visitors!

He slaps GEORGE on the back and laughs boyishly. GEORGE does his best to join in. WALLACE carries the laugh round to SARAH who also joins in.

★   ★   ★

ANDREW, a boy of six is standing by a birthday cake with six candles on it. He is dressed in a suit and tie and is perspiring. Several other children and the adult guests are grouped round ANDREW singing.

GUESTS: Happy Birthday to you,
                   Happy Birthday to you,
                   Happy Birthday, dear Andrew,
                   Happy Birthday to you . . .

GEORGE and SARAH who have been rather self-consciously singing with the others, smile with relief as the song seems to come to an end. However it doesn't and they have to join in again.

                   Oh, you're six years old today,
                   Six years old today,
                   You won't be five anymore,
                   But you've never been six years old before . . .

★   ★   ★

GEORGE, drink in hand, looks across the lounge to see SARAH, surrounded by a group of men and looking a little like the Queen on a Commonwealth visit. One of the men finishes a story and all the men laugh. SARAH joins in. GEORGE drinks.

★   ★   ★

GEORGE and SARAH are with MICHAEL, the young African they met earlier.

MICHAEL: You see, the Western so-called democracies, they totally and utterly misunderstand what we mean by the one-party state. It is not about people holding on to power . . . it is about creating one nation, that is all. We cannot afford the luxury of squabble and petty politics. If people are hungry and uneducated, what is politics compared to that? We do not have enough people of talent to let them split into parties and fight each other! Black, White, Shona, Matabele, we must work together for the good of the nation. That is what we mean by the one-party state. That is the theory, anyway . . . let us hope the practice works out as well.

He laughs, SARAH and GEORGE join in.

No, this country could be a wonderful country. Wonderful country. Oh, we often curse the British . . . but we know we have a debt to them. When the Portuguese left Mozambique, they switched off the light and took the light bulbs. At least the British left the light bulbs!

He laughs again.

(*through his laughter*) Only a joke, of course. A white judge told me that one!

50

★　　★　　★

GEORGE, SARAH and WALLACE are with WALLACE'S FATHER, a large man, probably in his sixties. WALLACE'S FATHER speaks in Shona, then nods to WALLACE to translate. GEORGE and SARAH listen as attentively to the Shona as they do to the translation.

WALLACE:　　　　　My father says that he is pleased that you may be working for me. It shows the right spirit, he says.

The FATHER speaks in Shona, then nods to WALLACE.

　　　　　　　　　He says that we were all very disappointed at the '85 elections to find many whites still voting for Smith, a racist who waged a useless war, imprisoned many people and committed many atrocities.

The heads turn to the FATHER again as he speaks in Shona, then nods. GEORGE and SARAH turn to WALLACE.

　　　　　　　　　He says the votes themselves do not matter because the white issue is dead and the separate voting roll will soon be abolished . . . but the fact that these people still support Smith shows that they still believe in the myth of white superiority — an attitude not to be tolerated in a free and independent Zimbabwe.

The heads turn, the FATHER speaks in Shona, nods, the heads turn back to WALLACE.

　　　　　　　　　It is obvious that you are different, he says . . . it is obvious that you are good Zimbabweans.

★　　★　　★

A Queen *record is playing on the music centre and several couples, including WALLACE and LINDA, are dancing disco style. SARAH and GEORGE stand at the side watching them.*

WALLACE: *(calling to them)* Join in . . . come on!

GEORGE laughs.

GEORGE: Oh, we're too old.

WALLACE: Nonsense!

GEORGE: Don't worry, we're quite happy watching you. *(then quietly, to SARAH)* Well I think we've done the necessary. Want to go?

★   ★   ★

GEORGE and SARAH, preparing to leave, are with WALLACE and LINDA.

WALLACE: Thank you so much for coming.

GEORGE: Thank you for asking us.

SARAH: We enjoyed it very much.

GEORGE: Oh yes. You must visit us sometime.

LINDA: Thank you. When shall we come?

GEORGE is aware of SARAH'S instinctive look at him.

GEORGE: Well . . . whenever you like . . . um . . .

WALLACE: I will fix it up with George. So then, George, about the other matter . . . perhaps we shouldn't talk business here, but all I want to say is . . .

He stops as something catches his eye.

> Oh Uncle!

They follow his look to see a well-dressed man in his sixties has come into the room. He is carrying a large gift-wrapped parcel.

> Uncle . . . so pleased you could come.

BADINGA:	Would I miss a birthday? Hullo Linda, my sweetheart, where's the birthday boy?
LINDA:	I'll fetch him, Uncle.
BADINGA:	Fetch him . . . fetch him!
WALLACE:	Uncle . . . let me introduce you to George and Sarah Beesley.
BADINGA:	I am most delighted to meet you. How do you do.

He holds out his hand. GEORGE takes it.

GEORGE:	Hullo.
BADINGA:	I've heard a lot about you from Wallace.
GEORGE:	*(laughing nervously)* Oh.
BADINGA:	Good reports. Good reports. And Mrs Beesley . . . most delighted.

BADINGA holds out his hand to her, her hesitation is slight but noticeable, then she takes his hand.

SARAH:	Hullo.
BADINGA:	What a lovely dress you're wearing.

SARAH: (quietly) Thank you.

ANDREW runs up to BADINGA.

BADINGA: Ah . . . here's the boy of the moment!

ANDREW: My present, Uncle . . . my present!

BADINGA: I haven't got you a present.

ANDREW: You have . . . give it me!

BADINGA: Oh there you are . . . go on!

ANDREW: Thank you . . . thank you . . .

He runs away with the parcel.

BADINGA: I can't deny boys anything. Have you boys,
                      Mrs Beesley?

SARAH: (icily) We had two. One was killed in the war.

BADINGA: I am so sorry. It's a terrible loss. A terrible
                      loss. Irreplaceable. At least you have one left.
                      Make the most of him. My three were killed.

GEORGE: (brief pause) I'm sorry.

BADINGA: War is a terrible thing.

He catches sight of WALLACE'S FATHER, who is sitting on a chair.

                      Ah, Moses . . . you old villain. (to the others)
                      Please excuse me.

GEORGE: Of course.

BADINGA: (moving off) Moses . . . how are you?

WALLACE'S FATHER answers in Shona.

> Oh come on, you old rogue . . . you speak
> English as well as I do.

WALLACE: *(smiling to GEORGE and SARAH)* He does, too. For some reason of his own he prefers not to!

GEORGE laughs uncomfortably.

GEORGE: Well . . . we must be going.

WALLACE: Yes, of course. I was going to say, George . . . about the business matter . . . it's up to you now.

GEORGE: Oh I see . . . good . . . fine . . . thank you.

WALLACE: Will you let me know on Monday?

GEORGE: Oh yes . . . definitely . . . yes.

SARAH watches as GEORGE beams and shakes hands with WALLACE.

> Thank you very much.

SCENE 17: IN THE CAR
FLASHBACK FEBRUARY 1986

It is now dark. GEORGE is driving a 25 year old Anglia. SARAH sits beside him.

GEORGE: Nice Mercedes in the drive.

She doesn't reply.

> All that talk about the hungry . . . don't
> suppose they go very hungry.

Still she says nothing.

Still . . . not too bad, was it?

SARAH: *(quietly)* No.

GEORGE: Pity he had to turn up at the end . . . but then . . . I suppose.

SARAH: He's his uncle.

GEORGE: Yes. And give him his due he was polite enough. I didn't realise he'd lost three kids. Puts it in perspective a bit.

She says nothing.

Wallace is all right though, isn't he?

SARAH: Yes.

GEORGE: And I thought the others were OK too. Talked some waffle, of course . . . but not like some you meet . . . nothing racist about them. Still early, want to call in at the club?

SARAH: Not me, no. You go if you want . . . drop me off at the house.

GEORGE: Don't think I'll bother.

He glances at her.

You did very well, I was proud of you.

SARAH: *(quietly)* Thank you.

GEORGE: And he offered me the job.

SARAH: Oh yes.

GEORGE: What do you think? Should I take it?

SARAH, after a brief pause and without looking at him.

SARAH: Only sensible thing to do.

GEORGE smiles then touches the dashboard.

GEORGE: Might even replace the jalopy now!

SARAH: (suddenly) Can you stop a minute?

GEORGE: What for?

SARAH: I don't feel very well.

GEORGE: Oh yes . . . of course.

SCENE 18: GEORGE AND SARAH'S HOUSE
FLASHBACK FEBRUARY 1986

The lounge is in darkness, then the lights are switched on and GEORGE comes into the room. He looks back towards the door uncertainly. SARAH comes to the door.

GEORGE: All right now?

SARAH: Yes fine . . . fine.

GEORGE: Those funny cakes, I daresay.

SARAH: Just the strain, I expect. Nerves always seem to affect my stomach.

GEORGE: Are a strain, these occasions. Still . . . you didn't look nervous. Looked cool as a cucumber.

She half-smiles.

	Well I'm going to have a drink.
SARAH:	I'll have a brandy and soda.
GEORGE:	You sure?
SARAH:	Always settles me.
GEORGE:	Right.

As he goes to the drinks trolley, she stands looking round the room, then, as they talk, she goes to the small desk, takes a key from the top drawer, opens a bottom drawer and takes out three framed photographs.

	Not too liberal with it there. Know what it's usually like with Afs . . . drink till it comes out of their ears.
SARAH:	It was a children's birthday party.
GEORGE:	Oh yes, quite right.

As they continue talking, she, unseen by him, ranges the photographs along the mantelpiece. The first is of GEORGE, with two young boys on either side of him, holding a fish which is so large that it stretches across the three bodies. The second photograph is another copy of the one we have already seen in PETER'S flat — PETER, PAUL and SARAH beside the swimming pool. The third is a straight portrait of PETER.

SARAH:	You'll make the arrangements, will you, for asking them here?
GEORGE:	Well . . . no hurry about that.
SARAH:	Can't leave it long . . . that'll get you off on the wrong foot entirely.
GEORGE:	I suppose you're right. I have a feeling that if I can keep on the right side, things might turn

out very well. Ask them for dinner then, shall we?

SARAH: Sure we're up to their standards for that?

GEORGE: Good Heavens yes . . . you're a very good . . .

He turns with the drinks, then stops as he sees the photographs.

                What you playing at?

SARAH: What's the matter?

GEORGE: You know I won't have those up.

SARAH: Look, there's no point in being silly, George. I went with you today . . . and I'm saying you're right. If we're saying that, we're saying Peter was right. We can't shut him out if we agree with him.

GEORGE: Well who the hell says I agree with him?

SARAH: Have you forgotten what he said?

SCENE 19: GEORGE AND SARAH'S HOUSE
FLASHBACK 1976

There is a rucksack on the floor beside PETER as he stands in the lounge facing GEORGE and SARAH. GEORGE and SARAH are dressed differently from the previous scene.

PETER: It's a useless war, Dad . . . and they're going to win. They've got to win because they're right. It's their country, not ours. They should be in charge . . . and very soon they will be in charge and you'll have to accept it.

GEORGE: That bloody lot? Don't be stupid!

PETER:	It's Smithy who's stupid. He can't win. You can't stop progress.
GEORGE:	Oh you know it all, don't you . . . you're talking like a soapbox . . . what are you? Eighteen?
PETER:	Eighteen. And I'm not killing them . . . and I'm not getting killed for some sort of cause that's wrong and hopeless. I'm getting out.
GEORGE:	You mean you're chicken. You're yellow. You're running 'cause you're scared.
PETER:	I'm sorry Dad . . . if that's . . .
GEORGE:	And what about Paul? He's out there now in the bush. He's fighting for his country. He's fighting for you. What d'you think about that?
PETER:	I don't know, Dad . . . I just know it's wrong and I think we should settle.
GEORGE:	Oh you do, do you, Mr. Intellect? Chuck it all . . . chuck our standards . . . chuck everything. Hand it over to the blacks. *Yes Sir, no Sir . . . you're the masters now!*
PETER:	They are the masters, Dad . . . or they very soon will be.
GEORGE:	Not in one bloody million years, chum!

Slight pause.

PETER:	I'm sorry, Dad . . . sorry, Mum.

SARAH looks from PETER to GEORGE, but says nothing.

GEORGE: You're due to report for training on Monday
                   next week. Are you going to be there?

PETER: I'm not. I'm getting out.

Another slight pause.

GEORGE: Very well.

He takes out his wallet, takes out some money from it and holds it out to
PETER.

                   There's sixty dollars . . . it's all I've got. For
                   your Mum's sake, I won't let you starve.

PETER: I don't want it.

GEORGE: Take it.

PETER: Thanks.

GEORGE: But once you take that chicken run, I don't
                   want to see you or hear of you again. As far
                   as we're concerned, you're finished. Dead.
                   You going to change your mind?

PETER shakes his head.

                   Get out.

PETER looks at them, then picks up the rucksack.

PETER: Bye Dad . . . bye Mum.

He goes out and closes the door behind him. SARAH stares at the door for a
moment, then begins to cry.

SCENE 20: PETER'S FLAT
MARCH 1986

GEORGE and PETER sit avoiding each other's eyes, each isolated in their own thoughts.

SCENE 21: GEORGE AND SARAH'S HOUSE
FLASHBACK FEBRUARY 1986

GEORGE and SARAH are in the lounge.

SARAH: He was right, wasn't he? It was all a waste of time. Paul needn't have died. Peter needn't have gone. They could both be still here. You'd've done what you're doing if we'd just given in.

GEORGE: For God's sake, I don't know what you're on about! You mean because I'm going to work for a black? We didn't fight the war 'cause we were anti-black!

SARAH: Didn't we?

GEORGE: *(quickly)* No! We fought for standards. That's what we fought for. That's what we stood for. We fought the riff-raff, the commies, we didn't fight the blacks. The white man in this country was never anti-black. There was no country in the whole of Africa where the blacks were treated as well as here. We didn't have apartheid . . . nothing like that. We had education . . . we had progress. We believed in the black man achieving his rights. You don't give rights to a man before he's ready for them. If you do your standards go to pot. Equal rights for equal people . . . that's what progress is about. Progress takes time. We fought the terrs 'cause they wouldn't take time. For fifteen years we made them take time. All right, they're not ready . . . but they're better than they were. And Wallace Badinga's better than most. And who made him what he is? You tell me that! We made him. Oh yes. So, who cares if I have to work for him! It's not saying the war was a waste to do that!

SARAH says nothing.

Here . . . come on, have your drink.

She takes the drink, sits down, then drinks.

SARAH: *(quietly)* I'm sorry . . . I didn't realise that. I mean . . . what the war was all about.

GEORGE: What did you think then?

SARAH: I suppose I thought . . . what you said. What I thought you said. I thought it was about . . . keeping our way of life. I mean, keeping what we had . . . keeping what we . . . what we'd worked for. About not having them in our areas. About not having them in our schools. About them being black and us being white. And us being different and better than they were.

GEORGE: Oh come on . . . you never thought that.

SARAH: It's what you *said*! Have you forgotten? Don't lie to *me*!

He says nothing.

                    (quiet again) I don't think at first I thought at all. I had a nice house, lovely kids . . . kids I

63

really loved . . . we were very happy, that's all I thought. I didn't think about blacks at all. I should've done, but I didn't. They were just there. Then you said they wanted to take what we'd got. They were getting above themselves, *you said* . . . we had to keep them in their place. They're only just out of the jungle, *you said* . . . half-civilised, *you said* . . . dirty, *you said* . . . and they don't know how to use lavatories. Never be fit to run a country, *you said*. Look at the shape of their heads, *you said* . . . and their lips, *you said* . . . not to mention the way they walk . . . they're nearer apes than men, *you said*. If we don't keep them under control then they'll go berserk and take all we've got and very soon ruin the country, *you said*.

GEORGE: For goodness sake . . . I never . . .

SARAH: It's what *you said!*

There is a brief silence.

That's what a lot of people said. Then Paul went to fight and we all cheered. Then Peter wouldn't fight and he went away . . . and Paul got killed . . . and Peter wouldn't come back for his funeral because if he did he'd still have to fight . . . and you said you'd given him a second chance and he hadn't taken it and that was the end, and I have never seen him since. So there we were. I'd lost both the boys. And most of what you said the blacks would take they'd already got as far as I was concerned. And all there was left of what you said was us being different and better than them. And I started to hate them. Perhaps I always had. You don't start something like that out of nothing. Perhaps it was only then I realised it.

Anyway, however it happened, that was it . . . it was there. I couldn't bear to be near them. I still can't. They make my flesh creep. And I may look stupid, but I'm not, and I realise it's wrong what I feel . . . it's disgusting what I feel . . . but I still feel it. Even there today. Those people today. Very nice . . . very hospitable. Much brainer than I am . . . no doubt about that. I can't seem to help it . . . I can't stand to be near them. I felt sorry for Badinga when he said about his kids, and he was very polite and all the rest . . . but I still couldn't bear being close to him. And it's nothing to do with the war any more . . . or even the fact they killed Paul . . . it's just . . . no answer . . . I can't stand blacks. And the thought of having them here in my house and you saying *yes Sir* . . . *no Sir* to them and arse crawling to them and . . .

GEORGE: Shut up! Shut up! Jesus Christ, what's the matter with you?

SARAH: *(quietly)* I'm sorry. I disgust myself. But please don't forget it's what you said. *(she drinks)* Well, you seem to have changed, so I can change. I've got to somehow and I will. And you've got to take that job. Good job . . . good opportunities. I didn't disgrace you today, did I?

GEORGE: No.

SARAH: Well I won't . . . I promise. It'll be all right.

She smiles at him. He half-smiles back.

                Let's snap out of it and go to the club.

GEORGE: You said you didn't want to go.

SARAH: Changed my mind!

SCENE 22: THE CLUB
FLASHBACK FEBRUARY 1986

An old-fashioned record player is playing Sinatra singing A Foggy Day in London Town. *At a table near the bar BRIAN is distributing glasses from a tray.*

BRIAN: So how was your auntie?

GEORGE: Auntie?

BRIAN: Sarah said you had to visit your auntie . . . stopped you coming to the lake.

GEORGE looks at SARAH.

SARAH: *(quickly)* Oh we had a change of plan after that . . . we had an invitation to a party.

CATHY: Oh, thank you very much!

SARAH: Well, we couldn't really refuse. It was sort of business. It was at Mr Badinga's house.

CATHY and BRIAN look at each other.

GEORGE: *(clarifying)* Badinga's nephew's house.

SARAH: Yes. It was his son's birthday and they were having a party and they asked us along.

CATHY: They asked you?

SARAH: Yes.

BRIAN: Trying to butter you up to work for him?

GEORGE:	*(uncomfortably)* I suppose so, yes.
CATHY:	*(anticipating good gossip)* And you went to a party? At his house? I mean, what was it like? What were they like?
SARAH:	It was very nice, wasn't it, George?
GEORGE:	Yes.
SARAH:	Lovely house. And they were charming. Absolutely charming. Weren't they, George?
GEORGE:	Yes.
CATHY:	Oh.
SARAH:	And Badinga himself turned up . . . and he was charming, wasn't he, George?
GEORGE:	Yes, he was . . . yes.
SARAH:	It was a very enjoyable occasion.
BRIAN:	Oh really?
SARAH:	Oh yes.

She drinks. They all drink. CATHY and BRIAN glance at each other uncomfortably, then as they glance at SARAH. SARAH finds herself half-smiling, half-winking, confidentially.

CATHY:	*(smiling)* Oh come on . . . you can tell *us*. What was it like?
SARAH:	It was fine, wasn't it, George?
GEORGE:	Yes.
CATHY:	And the rest . . . come on!

She is still smiling at SARAH. SARAH sniggers.

What is it?

SARAH: No, it's a bit sad, really. I was just thinking about that poor boy . . . their son. I know it rained a bit but it was still very hot and there he was, poor kid, best suit buttoned up, collar and tie, perspiration dripping right off him!

CATHY: *(laughing quietly)* Oh poor kid.

BRIAN: They have to overdo everything . . . even their kids they overdo!

CATHY: Just showing off.

As SARAH continues, GEORGE can only sit and watch.

SARAH: Well, if you want to talk about showing off, you should've seen their telly . . . bloomin' great colour telly on all through the party with the sound turned down!

BRIAN: *(laughing)* Just to prove they'd got one!

SARAH: And I tell you they couldn't have the sound up 'cause they never stopped talking . . . and the funny thing was if they weren't on about their videos, they were on about the one-party state . . . I mean, what are they? Commies or capitalists?

BRIAN: Capi-commies!

CATHY: *(laughing)* Dapi-commies!

SARAH: And the father . . . hang on . . . the father . . . *Yobba yobba yobba in Shona all the time . . . Yobba yobba yobba . . . translate, my son . . . my father, he says yobba yobba yobba!* And there was our heads going from one to the other like we were watching a tennis match!

CATHY, BRIAN and SARAH are now laughing freely. GEORGE watches them very uncomfortably.

Then they . . . no listen . . . then they gave us these cakes. *This is my wife's prize cooking,* he says. So I said to George, *You've got to eat it,* I said, *Go on . . . eat it.* You should've seen his face! And that's before he tried it. You should've seen it again when he got it in his mouth!

They are laughing even louder.

And then they started to dance . . . oh me, oh my! Whoo-whoo whoo-whoo *(she wiggles her shoulders)* Trying to look like they were on the disco floor. The only thought that went through my mind was *Bring out the tom-toms!*

BRIAN and CATHY roar with laughter. GEORGE is acutely embarrassed.

SCENE 23: GEORGE AND SARAH'S HOUSE
FLASHBACK FEBRUARY 1986

GEORGE comes into the lounge. Without concentrating on what he is doing he strolls across to an armchair, flops down and stares towards the dead television set. SARAH comes into the doorway and looks at him.

SARAH: Don't know why I said all that.

He doesn't reply.

                  I do disgust myself.

GEORGE: *(quietly)* Yes. You said.

She stands watching him, then looks away.

SARAH: I'm going to bed.

She goes out of the room. After a moment GEORGE gets out of his chair, goes to the mantelpiece and looks at the photographs which SARAH put there earlier. GEORGE'S eyes move from the picture of himself and the two boys holding the fish, to see the picture of SARAH, PETER and PAUL round the swimming pool.

SCENE 24: PETER'S FLAT
MARCH 1986

GEORGE and PETER are sitting as before.

GEORGE: Sunday the weather was very nice . . . not too
                        hot . . . nor rain . . . we were in the garden
                        most of the day. Didn't talk much. I don't
                        mean we were silent. I mean we just talked . . .
                        routine. Not about the job or Badinga at all.
                        In the evening we watched a bit of television
                        . . . Dynasty's on on Sunday . . . always
                        watch it if we're home. Monday morning I
                        went to work. It was Mr Pietmeyer's last
                        week. I had to telephone Baginda to tell him
                        what I was doing. Well, I didn't in the
                        morning, thought I'd do it in the afternoon.
                        'Bout two o'clock I got this phone call, from
                        our houseboy, Emmanuel. Don't know how
                        he found the number of where I worked.
                        Didn't even know he could use the phone.
                        Anyway, of course, I went straight home.

GEORGE stares into space.

70

SCENE 25: GEORGE AND SARAH'S HOUSE
FLASHBACK FEBRUARY 1986

SARAH is lying on the bed. EMMANUEL is standing by the bedside.

GEORGE'S VOICE: **She was lying on the bed, she could have been asleep. Her arm was hanging from her shoulder in an unnatural fashion. Two unstoppered bottles of pills, an open bottle of brandy and a glass were on the bedside table. Emmanuel was standing by the bedside.**

SCENE 26: PETER'S FLAT
MARCH 1986

GEORGE: We got an ambulance. Got her to hospital. It was too late, though. The doctor didn't think she'd really meant to . . . you know. Hadn't taken enough for that. Enough to send her to sleep, of course . . . then she . . . vomited and choked. Often happens, it seems.

PETER, has not moved, now for a moment he drops his eyes.

That was two weeks ago. Had to be an inquest. Then the funeral. I didn't have the guts to ask you to that.

He looks at PETER, but PETER is not looking at him. GEORGE gets up, goes to the mantelpiece and stares at the photograph of PETER, PAUL and SARAH.

Wasn't my fault, was it?

PETER doesn't answer. GEORGE has to look at him.

I mean, it wasn't my fault she felt that way. It wasn't was it, Pete?

PETER looks at him, then looks away.

PETER: *(quietly)* Poor Mum.

SCENE 27: WALLACE BADINGA'S OFFICE
APRIL 1986

Portraits of MUGABE and PRESIDENT BANANA now hang on the wall of the office.

WALLACE: Come in.

WALLACE sits behind the desk. The door opens and GEORGE comes into the office.

                          Ah, hullo George.

GEORGE: Good morning, Sir.

WALLACE: How are you feeling now?

GEORGE: Not too bad, Sir.

WALLACE: I'm glad to hear it. Sit down, George.

GEORGE: Thank you, Sir.

He sits.

WALLACE: Now George . . . things are going well . . .
                          but there's just one or two matters I'd like to
                          go over with you.

GEORGE: Yes Sir. Of course, Sir.

WALLACE spreads some papers on the desk.

APPENDIX

People often ask, "How do I become a television writer?"

Answer: "Sit down on a chair and move the pen across the paper until you have written something that interests you and you think will interest other people." You may be a genius and your first effort is a dream of a play; you may be more typical (like me) and finish five or six before you come up with anything that would excite anyone. Either way, you have to face the biggest hurdle — actually selling the first play. The script departments of the BBC and ITV receive thousands of unsolicited scripts a year. I'm sure the people who work there are very conscientious but they haven't the time to give full consideration to everything that comes through their letterbox. The temptation to flick through to page four . . . yawn . . . page twelve . . . yawn again and then dump the script in the reject basket, must be considerable. How many pearls go down the drain?

But, suppose you're lucky? Suppose your play takes the eye of a script editor or a producer? Suppose they utter the magic words: *We're going to buy it.* What happens then? Well, firstly, you're a professional, you're being paid and don't knock it, that's your bed and board. I once heard Alistair Cooke say that when he wanted to talk about art, he mixed with bankers and when he wanted to talk about money, he mixed with artists. A writer wants to be praised, but has to be paid.

A first play, produced and shown, and liked by some, is an enormous step forward. Then you reach the stage where you may be commissioned. Commissioning is a wonderful thing, it means that the company who commissions you, pay you a third, even half of the money to allow you to live while you write the play. You could, of course, say, *Thank you very much,* and scarper off to a Greek Island and never deliver a play at all. It's very tempting. The snag is that they are unlikely ever to commission anything else from you. Commissioning comes about in one of several ways. Perhaps you have an idea for a play, or a series and you meet a producer and tell him or her about it. If they like your idea (and they know your previous work), they will probably commission you to write it. Sometimes the producer has the idea and asks if you would be interested in making it into a play, or they have a novel they want adapted into a series, or a clip from a newspaper they want to base a drama on. Sometimes the producer simply has a drama slot to fill and will ring you up to ask if you have an idea. The golden rule here is never say *No*, say *Yes* and think up something before you meet them.

So the play, or series, or episode of a series is commissioned and you go away to write it. After that no two writers work in the same way. Until the time of production, the job (and if you make your living by it, it is a job) is about being alone. The two worst things about being a writer are the amount of time you have to spend alone and the amount of time you spend staring at a blank sheet of paper. Those feelings, I assume, all writers have in common. The details are individual. Some writers tell me they work on a word processor, some use a portable typewriter, some like me, use a 12p biro. Some plot the entire piece of work before they start. Others like me, start from the first line and are surprised by what follows. I find this way exciting and feel that if it surprises me, it surprises the viewer — not, unfortunately, always true. This method also has the drawback of meaning that the play you end up with may be nothing like the play you described to the producer. There is usually no problem if the producer happens to like the finished product, but there can be nasty recriminations if this doesn't happen to be the case.

Even television critics mix up the roles of the producer and the director. The producer is the person who puts the show together. He or she commissions the writer, decides if the play should be put into production, then chooses the director to direct it and is responsible for the money spent. The director is the person who chooses the cast, rehearses the actors and has the final say as to which pictures are seen on screen. The best producers consult the writer before appointing the director. This choice is very important, given that it is the director's job to realise the writer's play. Some directors, the best, are only too willing to work with writers. They try to ensure that what is seen on screen is as near as possible to the writer's intentions. There are directors who interpret their function very differently. (Like the film director *Joe Bloggs* who plants a camera in front of a writer's creation and has the nerve to call it *A Film By Joe Bloggs*, as if the whole thing is down to him. Writers have a corner in hell set aside for directors who do that). In between there are directors who feel that the writer should be read on paper but never heard in opinion. The writer tries to avoid both these types and, if once inflicted with them, puts a big cross against their name and vows never to work with them again.

The best, and I have worked with a good many of these, are a joy. I include here Jane Howell, who so brilliantly directed the television production of *Drums Along Balmoral Drive*. They consult the writer from the beginning, they want the writer to be at the casting sessions, at rehearsals and in the studio or on location. When you work with a director like this, the adrenalin races; this after all is what you have waited for. A novel is an entity in itself; a play is not fulfilled until actors give it flesh and blood. Of course there are bad actors, of course parts are misinterpreted. But when I sit at rehearsals — nothing matches the excitement of a creative rehearsal — and watch actors not only bringing the characters to life in the way I intended, but also adding the extra thrilling dimension of infusing their own personalities into the role, then I get the real kick that makes me want to carry on writing.

First nights on television are just as important to me as any first night in the theatre would be. The production is usually recorded and I have seen it probably several times, but the time it goes out is still very special because several million people are seeing it at the same time. A show in the West End would have to play to full houses every night for twenty years, to be seen by as many people as watch the average television play. When the credits roll, you wait for the telephone calls from your friends. Did they like it? Well, they say they did. That's what friends are for. The public need not be so sensitive. After one of my first television plays I went round to the newsagent next morning to collect the papers:

"Hey," he said, "didn't you write that play last night?"

"Yes," I said modestly.

"Wasn't it rotten?" he said. I could think of no answer. I smiled. "No, seriously," he said, "didn't you think it was rotten?"

I smiled again, paid for the papers and went home to try for better luck next time.

Douglas Livingstone

ZIMBABWE — A Summary of Historical and Political Events

5th century
Ancestors of Shona (Mashona) speaking Zimbabweans settle on land between the Zambezi and Limpopo rivers.

13th-15th century
The building of Great Zimbabwe, the capital of the great Shona state. Zimbabwe means *a burial ground of chiefs*.

1850s
Ndebele (Matabele) people settle in southern part of the country, north of Limpopo river.

1890
Cecil Rhodes founds the British South Africa Company. This part of Africa is named Rhodesia by Europeans. South Africa Company troops (The Pioneers) occupy Mashonaland, home of Shona people.

1896-97
Hostilities (the first Chiremunga) take place between Africans and white settlers, resulting in white occupation of Matabele (Ndebele) territory. The conquest of Rhodesia is complete.

1922
Whites vote for self-government under British control and reject union with South Africa.

1924
First election in Rhodesia. Electoral roll contains only a few hundred black voters. British South Africa Company concludes its rule.

1925
British settlers' policy of white supremacy formed.

1930
Land Apportionment Act gives white minority 50% of land. Africans earn low salaries as labourers, insecure tenants for whites. 'Homeless' Africans are resettled on 'native reserves'.

1945+
Post war immigration strengthens position of European settlers.

1940-50
Labour Movement begins: Union of Railway Workers led by Joshua Nkomo, Teachers' Associations led by Rev. Ndabaningi Sithole and Robert Mugabe.

1951
Land Husbandry Act stops communal ownership of land, depriving many Africans of their livelihood.
A succession of franchise bills (1951, 1957, 1960) increase white political predominance.

1953
Inauguration of Federation of Rhodesia and Nyasaland.

1957	First Zimbabwean Nationalist party formed — the African National Congress with Nkomo as leader.
1959	African National Congress banned by ruling Federal party.
1960	National Democratic Party (NDP) formed, headed by Nkomo.
1961	NDP banned. Nkomo forms Zimbabwe African People's Union (ZAPU) (membership predominantly Ndebele.) The name Zimbabwe is adopted by Africans for country on black majority rule.
1962	ZAPU banned. White voters elect Rhodesian Front, a new right-wing party committed to white rule, under Winston Field.
1963	Nkomo attempts to set up a government in exile in Dar es Salaam. Sithole and Mugabe form the Zimbabwe African National Union (ZANU) (membership predominantly Shona) within Rhodesia.
1964	Rhodesian Government uses violent methods in African townships, resulting in clashes between Nationalists and police. ZANU banned. Nkomo, Mugabe and Sithole are detained without trial. Ian Smith becomes Prime Minister of Rhodesia. Labour Government elected in Britain under Harold Wilson.
1965	With support of South Africa and Portugal, Smith announces Unilateral Declaration of Independence (UDI). The intention — to perpetuate white settler minority rule for ever. Selective sanctions are applied by the United Nations.
1966	First guerrilla action undertaken by ZANU's military wing ZANLA (backed by China). Wilson meets Smith for talks on HMS Tiger.
1968	Wilson meets Smith for more talks on HMS Fearless. Further sanctions applied by United Nations against Rhodesia. The British Government states that there can be no Independence without black majority rule as a long-term aim. Smith refuses to accept this.
1969	Rhodesian voters accept a new constitution. Racial segregation intensifies.

1970	Rhodesia declares itself a Republic. In Britain the Conservative Party under Edward Heath wins the general election. British Government offers terms for a settlement in Rhodesia, similar to Wilson's. Smith accepts. Opposition to the settlement is spear-headed by the African National Council, led by Bishop Abel Muzorewa.
1972	The Pearce Commission: settlement rejected by Africans. Guerrilla hostilities intensify.
1974	Mozambique achieves Independence from Portugal. Rhodesia is no longer a viable buffer zone for South Africa. Mozambique provides bases for ZANLA, and ZIPRA — the Russian backed military wing of ZAPU. Most adult white males are now conscripted for at least part-time service in defence forces. Whites begin to emigrate.
1975	Talks between Smith and Nationalists lead to Lusaka Agreement. Nkomo and Mugabe are released, but ceasefire collapses. Mugabe flees to Mozambique to lead ZANU forces.
1976	Alarmed by deteriorating economic and military situation, USA forces Smith to accept black majority rule in principle. Britain fails to resolve hostilities at the Geneva Conference. Nkomo and Mugabe unite ZAPU and ZANU in the Patriotic Front (PF).
1977	New terms are thrown up by Britain and USA. Smith rejects them, but agrees to one man, one vote. Massive raids into Mozambique leave 1000 dead, mainly civilians. Smith starts talks with Sithole, Muzorewa and Chief Chirau to reach an internal settlement.
1978	Salisbury Agreement leads to a transitional government of Smith, Muzorewa, Sithole and Chirau. Mugabe and Nkomo oppose it. Viscount Air Disaster near Kariba. Ten of the eighteen survivors are shot as they await rescue in the Bush.
1979	Muzorewa wins general election under the Internal Settlement and becomes the first black Prime Minister of Zimbabwe Rhodesia. But he fails to end the war or carry out internal reforms. In Britain, the Conservative party under Margaret Thatcher wins the general election. The Commonwealth leaders conference in Lusaka proposes an Independence Conference involving Smith, Muzorewa and

the PF.
Lancaster House Conference opens in London in
September. An agreement is reached on a new constitution
and new elections. On December 12th Lord Soames arrives
in Salisbury as Governor for the transition. A
Commonwealth monitory force supervises a ceasefire.

1980   Mugabe's ZANU PF wins the elections. Independence and
black majority rule achieved. Rev. Canaan Banana is
Zimbabwe's first black President. Nkomo is appointed
Minister of Home Affairs.

1981   Nkomo demoted to Minister Without Portfolio. Mugabe's
party headquarters are destroyed in a bomb attack — six
killed, many injured.

1982   Tribal rivalries lead to sporadic fighting in Matabeleland.
Mugabe sacks Nkomo and two other ZAPU ministers after
a cache of arms is discovered on the property of Nkomo's
supporters.
Nine Whites leave Rhodesian Front. Chris Anderssen is
one of the two appointed to Mugabe's cabinet.

1983   Mugabe arrests Muzorewa as a threat to Zimbabwe's
security.

1984   Muzorewa freed.

1985   Elections result in another victory for Mugabe. Cabinet re-
shuffle retains Anderssen as the only white minister.
Mugabe resolves to abolish reserved seats for whites.

1986   Merger of ZANU-PF and ZAPU seen as a long-term aim.
Land Acquisition Act passed to speed up resettlement
without breaking the rules of the Lancaster House
Agreement.
Border hostilities — African National Congress premises
attacked by South Africans. Further attacks are made on
Zambia and Botswana.
National state of emergency announced in July. Internal
unity becomes a priority.

1987   Abolition of reserved white seats in Parliament. ZANU and
ZAPU agree to merge. Mugabe sworn in as Zimbabwe's
first executive President. Nkomo named as one of the two
vice-presidents of the newly amalgamated party. One white
minister and two white deputy ministers are given places
in the cabinet.

| 1988 | Nkomo becomes one of three senior ministers in the President's office. Mugabe declares one-party state attainable within three years. |

Note: Every effort has been made to ensure that the facts presented here are correct.

BIBLIOGRAPHY
A Brief History of Zimbabwe , Zimbabwe High Commission.
The Past is Another Country Rhodesia: UDI to Zimbabwe
  by **Martin Meredith,** Pan Books Limited.
None But Ourselves. Masses vs Media in the Making of Zimbabwe
  by **Julie Frederikse,** Zimbabwe Publishing House.
A History of South and Central Africa by **Derek Wilson,**
Cambridge University Press.
Africa Since 1800 by **Roland Oliver and Anthony Atmore,**
Cambridge University Press.

The editor and publishers would like to thank Adrian Holmes
and Andy Whittle for their help in compiling this section.